Alexander Hamilton

Libby Romero

NATIONAL
GEOGRAPHIC

Washington, D.C.

For Skye —L.R.

Library of Congress Cataloging-in-Publication Data
Names: Romero, Libby, author.
Title: Alexander Hamilton / by Libby Romero.
Description: Washington, DC : National Geographic Kids, 2018. | Series: National geographic reader | Includes index.
Identifiers: LCCN 2017020434 (print) | LCCN 2017026903 (ebook) | ISBN 9781426330407 (e-book) | ISBN 9781426330414 (e-book + audio) | ISBN 9781426330384 (pbk.) | ISBN 9781426330391 (hardcover)
Subjects: LCSH: Hamilton, Alexander, 1757-1804--Juvenile literature. | Statesmen--United States--Biography--Juvenile literature. | United States--Politics and government--1783-1809--Juvenile literature.
Classification: LCC E302.6.H2 (ebook) | LCC E302.6.H2 R66 2018 (print) | DDC 973.4092 [B] --dc23
LC record available at https://lccn.loc.gov/2017020434

The author and publisher gratefully acknowledge the expert content review of this book by Richard Sylla, chairman of the Museum of American Finance and professor emeritus of economics at New York University's Stern School of Business, and the literacy review of this book by Mariam Jean Dreher, professor of reading education, University of Maryland, College Park.

National Geographic supports K–12 educators with ELA Common Core Resources. Visit natgeoed.org/commoncore for more information.

Table of Contents

Who Was Alexander Hamilton?   4

A Challenging Childhood   6

In His Time   10

Coming to America   12

Revolutionary Change   18

A Passion for Politics   24

The New Nation   30

6 Cool Facts About Hamilton   34

The Deadly Duel   36

A Place in History   40

Quiz Whiz   44

Glossary   46

Index   48

Who Was Alexander Hamilton?

In His Own Words

"I would die to preserve the law upon a solid foundation; but take away liberty, and the foundation is destroyed."

Alexander Hamilton was one of the Founding Fathers of the United States of America. Even though he had a difficult childhood, he became a Revolutionary War hero, an important politician (pol-uh-TISH-un), and the founder of our country's financial (fuh-NAN-shul) system.

Hamilton never ran for president. But his ideas helped shape the new nation. He pushed for having a strong federal government. He set up a banking system that helped the young country survive. Many of his ideas are still used today.

Words to Know

POLITICIAN: A person who is involved in politics, which is the work of the government

FINANCIAL: Having to do with managing money for a person, company, or government

FEDERAL: Having to do with a central government that shares power with individual states

A Challenging Childhood

Hamilton was born on January 11 on Nevis (NEE-vus), a Caribbean island in the British West Indies. The exact year of his birth is unknown. Hamilton had two sets of birth records. One said he was born in 1755. The other said he was born in 1757, which is the date Hamilton used.

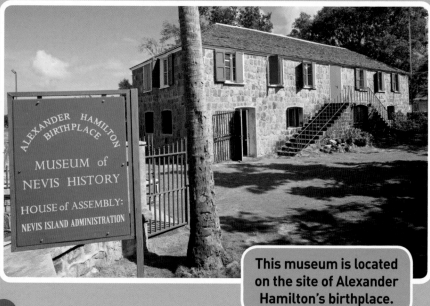

This museum is located on the site of Alexander Hamilton's birthplace.

Nevis is a round island formed around a big volcano called Nevis Peak. The island is surrounded by coral reefs.

Back then, Nevis was a colony of Great Britain. About 1,000 British colonists lived there. They grew sugar and sent ships to trade with far-off places.

Surrounded by Slavery

On Nevis, many people owned slaves. About 8,000 slaves were brought in to work on the sugar plantations. Hamilton saw owners treat slaves very badly. He hated what he saw. As an adult, Hamilton tried to get laws passed to end slavery in the United States.

Word to Know

COLONY: A land ruled by another country. The people who live there, called colonists, are subjects of the ruling country.

Hamilton's life was hard. His family was very poor. Also, his parents were never able to marry. His mother, Rachel, had married at age 16. But her husband treated her badly, so she left him. Then she met Hamilton's father, James. They had two children, Alexander and his older brother, James Jr.

St. Croix is another island in the West Indies. This photo shows the town where Hamilton grew up, as it appears today.

In 1765, the family moved to St. Croix (KROY). Soon after, Hamilton's father left and never returned. To make money, his mother opened a small store. Hamilton began working for the traders who brought goods for her to sell. But two years later, his mother died. Hamilton and James Jr. went to live with a cousin and then with an uncle. Within two years, both the cousin and the uncle died. Now the brothers, just young teens, were all alone.

That's a FACT! Hamilton didn't like to talk about his childhood. He was embarrassed by his humble beginnings.

In His Time

Hamilton grew up in the West Indies during the mid-1700s. Back then, many things were different from how they are today.

SCHOOL: Some children attended schools in churches. Children from wealthy families were sent to Europe, Canada, or the American colonies to complete their education.

TRADE: Sugar, which people called "white gold," and slavery were the biggest businesses. Today, most money in the region comes from tourism.

WORK AND PLAY: Children did many chores to help their families. But when they had free time, they played with homemade toys such as jump ropes, corn-husk dolls, and clay marbles.

Cuba, in the West Indies

GOVERNMENT: The islands of the West Indies were colonies held by several European countries. Today, most are independent nations.

CLOTHING: As babies, both boys and girls wore white dresses. But by the age of three, children started dressing like little adults. Girls wore tight, stiff dresses. Boys wore suits.

Coming to America

Hamilton faced many hardships. But instead of giving up, he worked hard to improve his life.

After their uncle's death, James Jr. got a job with a carpenter, and Hamilton kept working as a clerk. As part of his job, Hamilton ordered supplies. He handled money. He also charted courses for the ships that carried the company's supplies. Older businessmen were impressed with his skills. One of them even invited Hamilton to live with his family.

Hamilton worked as a clerk for the trading company that had brought goods to his mother's store. The goods often arrived on ships like this.

Another person Hamilton impressed was a minister named Hugh Knox (HYOO NOKS). Hamilton wrote poems and published them in the local newspaper. Knox noticed his poems and encouraged him to write more.

One day Hamilton wrote a letter about a recent hurricane. He showed the letter to Knox. Knox told Hamilton to publish it.

Hamilton as a teenager

In His Own Words

"The roaring of the sea and wind, ... the crash of the falling houses, and the ear-piercing shrieks of the distressed, were sufficient to strike astonishment into Angels."

—From Hamilton's letter about the hurricane, September 6, 1772

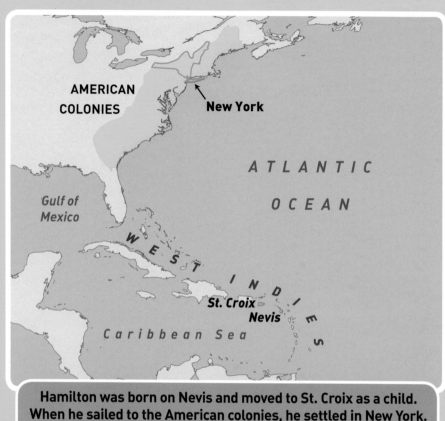

AMERICAN COLONIES

New York

ATLANTIC OCEAN

Gulf of Mexico

WEST INDIES

St. Croix

Nevis

Caribbean Sea

Hamilton was born on Nevis and moved to St. Croix as a child. When he sailed to the American colonies, he settled in New York. (Note: This map shows the colony borders as they were in 1772.)

People were amazed that a teenager could write so well. Local businessmen decided to send Hamilton to the American colonies to get a proper education. So in October 1772, Hamilton boarded a ship. He sailed off to the beginning of a better life.

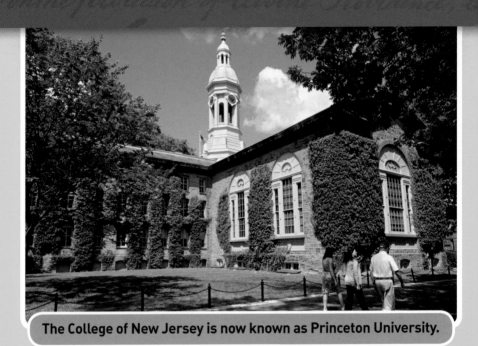

The College of New Jersey is now known as Princeton University.

Hamilton planned to enroll in the College of New Jersey. But when he reached the American colonies, he found he wasn't prepared to pass the school's hard entrance exam.

During the next year, he prepared for the test and passed it. But most people Hamilton's age had already finished college. He was just beginning. He asked to study at a faster pace in order to catch up. The college refused.

Hamilton decided to go to King's College in New York City instead. There, he could earn his degree more quickly.

Hamilton enrolled in King's College. Today it is known as Columbia University.

Hamilton Hall at Columbia University

Revolutionary Change

When Hamilton was in college, the American colonies were on the brink of war with Great Britain. Politics quickly became Hamilton's new passion. He spoke at rallies. He published papers supporting the American fight.

While at King's College, Hamilton spoke out about America's fight for independence.

Loyalists vs. Patriots

Colonists had different views during the Revolutionary War. Loyalists were people who wanted America to remain a colony of Great Britain. They were loyal to King George III. Patriots wanted to be free from British rule. They wanted the 13 colonies to govern themselves as an independent nation.

King George III

Hamilton never finished college. After the Revolutionary War began in April 1775, he joined a militia (muh-LISH-uh). He fought in battles and studied military plans. In early 1776, he became a captain in New York's state army.

Word to Know

MILITIA: A group of citizens organized for military service

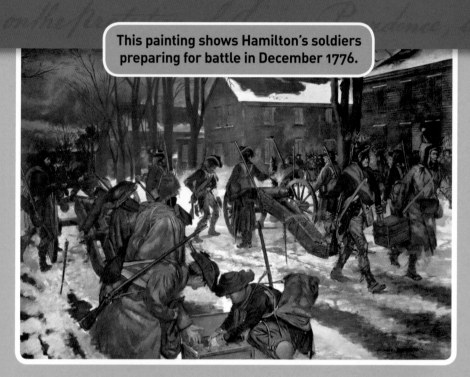

This painting shows Hamilton's soldiers preparing for battle in December 1776.

Hamilton was a fearless soldier. But he was an even better manager. He was organized and knew how to get the supplies his soldiers needed. George Washington, who was commander of the Continental Army, noticed this. In 1777, he asked Hamilton to join the Continental Army as his assistant.

Hamilton helped Washington plan battles and manage staff. He also wrote important letters. Many of those letters went to the Continental Congress, asking for food and other supplies for the troops.

General Washington asked a young Hamilton to join his staff.

While the troops fought for freedom, the Congress tried to figure out how to run the new country. As Washington's assistant, Hamilton watched the Congress struggle. Too many members were fighting for the rights of individual states. Hamilton thought the United States needed a strong federal government, too. He feared the nation would never succeed unless all the states came together as a union.

After four years on Washington's staff, Hamilton quit. He wanted to return to the battlefield. In 1781, his troops helped the Continental Army win the battle at Yorktown.

In His Own Words

"There is a certain enthusiasm in liberty, that makes human nature rise above itself in acts of bravery and heroism."

Yorktown was the last big battle of the Revolutionary War.

That's a FACT! At Yorktown, Hamilton became a famous hero when he led his soldiers on a night raid of one of the enemy's forts. They captured it in just 10 minutes.

A Passion for Politics

During the war, Hamilton met and married Elizabeth Schuyler (SKY-lur). After Yorktown, he retired from the military and joined her in Albany, New York. Their son Philip was born soon after. Philip was the first of eight children.

Elizabeth Schuyler Hamilton was also known as Eliza.

During the war, the Congress often met in the Pennsylvania State House, now known as Independence Hall.

Not one to sit still, Hamilton began to study law. For six months, he studied a friend's law books. Then he took and passed the bar exam. To Hamilton, becoming a lawyer wasn't just a job. It was the quickest way to get into politics. Many members of the Congress were lawyers.

That's a FACT! The bar exam is a test people must take to become lawyers. It takes most people three years of study to pass the exam.

In His Own Words

"Those who stand for
nothing fall for anything."

In 1782, the Hamilton family moved to New York City. Hamilton became a federal tax collector. His job was difficult. Many New Yorkers didn't want to pay taxes to the federal government. They wanted to keep money in their own state.

Hamilton knew this was a problem. The war was costing the country a lot of money. Some states paid their share, but others didn't. The federal government had to borrow money to pay the war debts (DETS).

That year, Hamilton was chosen to serve in the Continental Congress. He explained the problem to delegates from other states. But they wanted to keep tax money in their states, too.

Word to Know

DELEGATE: A person chosen to act for or represent others

Hamilton argued that the answer to this problem was to rewrite the Articles of Confederation. That was America's first constitution. He thought the document was weak. It gave too much power to the states and not enough to the federal government. After the war ended in 1783, more people began to listen.

This drawing shows Hamilton (center) speaking to Ben Franklin about the new constitution in 1787.

Hamilton wrote 51 of the 85 essays that explained the new constitution. Together, the 85 essays are known as *The Federalist Papers.*

At the Constitutional Convention in 1787, Hamilton and other delegates wrote a new constitution. Many delegates didn't like it. So Hamilton and two other leaders wrote essays explaining what it was and why it was needed. They convinced delegates to sign the new constitution.

Word to Know

CONSTITUTION: A set of laws by which a country is governed

The New Nation

As secretary of the Treasury, Hamilton (center) was one of several trusted advisers to President Washington (left). Together, the advisers were called the Cabinet.

In 1789, George Washington became the first U.S. president. Washington wanted to work with people he could trust. He asked Hamilton to be his secretary of the Treasury.

Hamilton started by dealing with America's war debts. To do that, he combined the federal debt with the remaining state debts. Then he used federal money to begin paying off the total debt. Hamilton also created the First Bank of the United States. The bank held the government's money. It also printed paper money.

the First Bank of the United States

Hamilton served as secretary of the Treasury until 1795. Washington left office two years later. Many people in the government neither liked nor trusted Hamilton. They were happy Hamilton was no longer in office.

The conflict with France ended before it turned into a war, but there was fighting at sea. In one famous battle, the U.S.S. *Constellation* (left) captured a French ship near Nevis.

In His Own Words

"People sometimes attribute my success to my genius; all the genius I know anything about is hard work."

But soon these people needed Hamilton. It seemed likely that America would go to war with France. Washington was asked to lead the troops. He agreed, but only if Hamilton was second in command. Hamilton was excited to lead troops into battle, but he never got the chance. In late 1800, the United States and France signed a peace agreement.

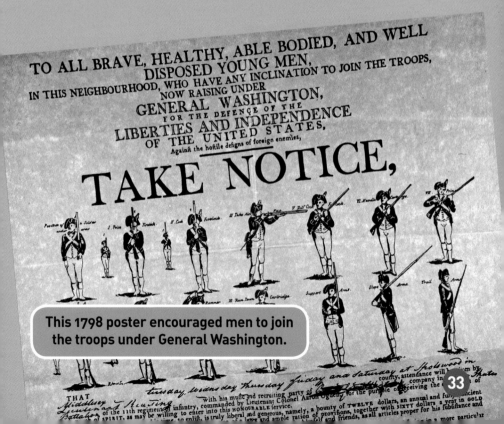

This 1798 poster encouraged men to join the troops under General Washington.

6 COOL FACTS About Hamilton

1

When Hamilton's mother died, the courts sold all her belongings to pay her medical bills. That included the books Hamilton loved to read. His uncle bought the books back for him.

2

As a young captain in the military, Hamilton was extremely focused and brave. Because of this, people called him the Little Lion.

3

Hamilton wrote most of George Washington's Farewell Address. In it, Washington announced he would not run for a third term as president. It is one of the most famous messages from a U.S. president.

Hamilton wrote many love poems for his wife. She kept one poem in a little bag that she wore around her neck until she died at age 97.

4

5

In 1801, Alexander Hamilton founded the *New-York Evening Post*. Now known as the *New York Post*, it is the 13th oldest newspaper in the United States.

Hamilton took part in nearly a dozen duels (DOO-ulz). All were with fellow politicians. And all but the final one were settled before either man fired a shot.

6

Word to Know

DUEL: A formal fight between two people to settle a disagreement. It is fought with weapons and often witnessed by others.

The Deadly Duel

There were many people who disagreed with Hamilton. One was a lawyer and politician named Aaron Burr.

Hamilton didn't trust Burr. So when Burr and Thomas Jefferson tied in the election for president in 1800, Hamilton spoke out against Burr. Jefferson was elected, and Burr became his vice president. When Burr ran for governor of New York four years later, Hamilton spoke out and Burr lost again.

Burr was angry. He needed a way to fix his career. So he challenged Hamilton to a duel. Hamilton accepted.

Aaron Burr was the third vice president of the United States.

The duel was set for July 11, 1804, in Weehawken, New Jersey. Hamilton and Burr met on a remote cliff that was surrounded by boulders and large trees.

At exactly 7 a.m., the men stood 10 paces apart. They announced that they were ready. And then, with an explosion of fire, they shot their pistols. Hamilton missed on purpose. Burr didn't. His shot hit Hamilton just above his right hip. Burr fled the scene. Hamilton died the next day.

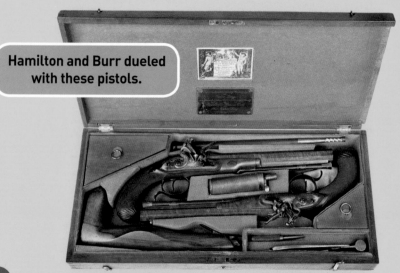

Hamilton and Burr dueled with these pistols.

Aaron Burr was charged with murder after killing Alexander Hamilton in the duel. The charges were later dropped.

An Honorable Duel

In 1801, Hamilton's oldest son, Philip, was challenged to a duel. Hamilton told his son that duels were about honor, and honorable men didn't shoot first. Philip took his father's advice, and he was shot and killed.

Philip Hamilton

A Place in History

Alexander Hamilton lived for less than 50 years. But in his short life, he made many important contributions to his young country. Hamilton's ideas about government helped shape the new nation. His financial wisdom helped the country survive.

The banking system Hamilton created still exists. So does the constitution he convinced the delegates to pass. And the system of government that he so strongly believed in is still used today.

1755/1757	1765	1766	1768
Born on Nevis on January 11; the exact year is unknown	His family moves to St. Croix	Begins working as a clerk	His mother dies

A statue of Hamilton stands outside the Treasury Building in Washington, D.C.

1772

Leaves for the American colonies

1773

Enrolls in King's College

1776

Becomes a captain in New York's state army

1777–1781

Serves on General Washington's staff in the Continental Army

Hamilton's wife, Elizabeth, wanted her husband's life to be remembered. So after he died, she collected his letters and papers. She hired people to write his life story. But she died before it was done. Their son John finally finished the biography in 1854.

That's a FACT!

In 2015, the U.S. Treasury announced that it was taking Alexander Hamilton off the $10 bill. Both historians and fans of the Broadway musical *Hamilton* protested. In 2016, the decision was reversed.

1780

Marries Elizabeth Schuyler

1781

Fights at Yorktown

1782

Studies law; serves in the Continental Congress

1787

Attends the Constitutional Convention; begins writing *The Federalist Papers*

The award-winning musical *Hamilton* uses rap and hip-hop music to tell the story of Hamilton's life.

Today, we honor Hamilton in many ways. His face is on the U.S. $10 bill. A musical about his life is a Broadway hit. More people than ever are learning about this early American who helped create the United States as we know it.

1789–1795

Serves as secretary of the Treasury

1801

His oldest son, Philip, is killed in a duel

1804

Fights a duel with Aaron Burr on July 11; dies in New York City on July 12

QUIZ WHIZ

How much do you know about Alexander Hamilton? After reading this book, probably a lot! Take this quiz and find out.

Answers are at the bottom of page 45.

Where was Alexander Hamilton born?

A. St. Croix
B. New York
C. Nevis
D. Great Britain

What was Hamilton's job as a child?

A. farmer
B. clerk
C. carpenter
D. minister

Why did Hamilton go to the American colonies?

A. to fight in the war
B. to become a banker
C. to see his parents
D. to get an education

4

During the Revolutionary War, Hamilton worked for _____.

A. Thomas Jefferson
B. Hugh Knox
C. George Washington
D. King George III

5

Hamilton helped write essays so delegates would pass _____.

A. the Articles of Confederation
B. the Bill of Rights
C. the Declaration of Independence
D. the Constitution

6

What did Hamilton do as secretary of the Treasury?

A. He combined the federal and state war debts.
B. He began paying off America's war debts.
C. He created the First Bank of the United States.
D. He did all of the above.

Who killed Alexander Hamilton?

A. Ben Franklin
B. Aaron Burr
C. George Washington
D. Thomas Jefferson

7

Glossary

AMERICAN COLONIES

New York

Gulf of Mexico

ATL

O C

COLONY: A land ruled by another country. The people who live there, called colonists, are subjects of the ruling country.

CONTINENTAL CONGRESS: The governing body of the American colonies during the Revolutionary War

DELEGATE: A person chosen to act for or represent others

FINANCIAL: Having to do with managing money for a person, company, or government

MILITIA: A group of citizens organized for military service

CONSTITUTION:
A set of laws by which
a country is governed

CONTINENTAL ARMY:
The official military group of
the American colonies during
the Revolutionary War

DUEL: A formal fight between
two people to settle a disagreement.
It is fought with weapons and often
witnessed by others.

FEDERAL: Having to do with a
central government that shares
power with individual states

POLITICIAN: A person who is
involved in politics, which is the
work of the government

SECRETARY OF THE TREASURY:
The leader of the U.S.
government department that
handles the country's money

Index

Boldface indicates illustrations.

A

Articles of Confederation 28

B

Banking system 5, 31, 40
Burr, Aaron 36–39, **37, 39**

C

Colony 7, 46
Constitution, U.S. 28–29, 40, **47**
Continental Army 20–22, 47, **47**
Continental Congress 21–22, 25, 27–28, 46, **46**

D

Delegate 27, 46, **46**
Duels **35,** 35–39, **38, 39,** 47, **47**

F

Federal 5, 47
Financial 5, 46
Franklin, Benjamin **28**

G

George III, King (England) 19, **19**

H

Hamilton (musical) 42, 43, **43**
Hamilton, Alexander
    on $10 bill 42, **42,** 43
    childhood 6–9
    college 16–18, **17**
    coming to America **12–13,** 12–17
    and Constitution **28,** 28–29, 40
    in Continental Congress 27–28
    cool facts 34–35, **34–35**
    death 38, **39**
    duels **35,** 35–39, **38, 39**
    in his time 10–11, **10–11**
    importance 4–5, 40
    as lawyer 25
    marriage 24, 35
    newspaper 35
    parents 8–9, 34
    passion for politics 24–29
    Revolutionary War **18,** 18–23, **20, 21, 23**
    as secretary of the Treasury 30–31, **31, 41**
    as tax collector 27
    as teenager 13–15, **14**
    U.S. conflict with France **32,** 33
    writing ability 14–15, 34–35
Hamilton, Elizabeth Schuyler (wife) 24, 35, **35,** 42
Hamilton, James, Jr. (brother) 8–9, 13
Hamilton, John (son) 42
Hamilton, Philip (son) 24, 39, **39**

J

Jefferson, Thomas 36

K

Knox, Hugh 14

M

Map 15
Militia 19, 46

N

Nevis (island) 6–7, **7**
New-York Evening Post 35, **35**

P

Politician 5, 47

Q

Quiz 44–45, **44–45**

R

Revolutionary War **18,** 18–23, **20, 21, 23,** 27, 31, 47, **47**

S

Secretary of the Treasury 30–31, **31, 41,** 47
Slavery 7, 10
St. Croix (island) **8–9,** 9

T

Timeline 40–43

W

Washington, George 20–22, **21,** 30, **30,** 33, 34, **34**
West Indies 6–11, **7, 8–9, 10–11**